Wild Stunts

STUNNING
MOTORCYCLE
STUNTS

by Tyler Omoth

Edge Books are published by Capstone Press,
1710 Roe Crest Drive, North Mankato, Minnesota 56003
www.capstonepub.com

Library of Congress Cataloging-in-Publication Data
Cataloging-in-publication information is on file with the Library of Congress.
ISBN 978-1-4914-4255-5 (library binding)
ISBN 978-1-4914-4316-3 (eBook PDF)

Editorial Credits
Nate LeBoutillier, editor; Kyle Grenz, designer; Jo Miller, media researcher;
Tori Abraham, production specialist

Photo Credits
Corbis: Bettmann, 6, Bo Bridges, 21; Courtesy of Ruth Fisher, 8; Denver Post via
Getty Images/Hyoung Chang, 23; Getty Images: The LIFE Picture Collection/Ralph
Crane, 19; Newscom: Icon SMI/Shelly Castellano, 12-13, imageBROKER/Jacek
Bilski, 11, Reuters/India/Stringer, 14-15, ZUMA Press/Gene Blevins, 24-25, ZUMA
Press/Martin Philbey, 20; Red Bull via Getty Images: Chris Tedesco, 5, Rich Van
Every, 28-29; Rex Features via AP Images, 27; Shutterstock: Christian Bertrand, 16-17,
Ivan Garcia, cover; The Image Works: Mirropix, 9, Scherl/SZ Photo, 7; The Kobal
Collection: CAROLCO, 26

Design Elements
Shutterstock: antishock, Igorsky, Leigh Prather, Kopirin, Radoman Durkovic

Direct Quotations
Page 14, from July 13, 2009 *ESPN* article "Robbie Maddison jumps Tower Bridge in
London," xgames.espn.go.com.
Page 19, from November 20, 2007, *Esquire* article "What I've Learned: Evel Knievel,"
www.esquire.com.
Page 24, from *The Daily Epic* article "This motorcyclist was paid $2 million to do the
craziest stunt of all time," www.thedailyepic.com.
Page 26, from *Entertainment Weekly* article "The art of motorcycle mayhem" by
Frank Spotnitz, www.ew.com.

Printed in the United States of America in North Mankato, Minnesota.
032015   008823CGF15

Table of Contents

Flying Into the Record Books

Sitting on your bike in front of a *quarter pipe*, you see the crowd through your helmet. They cheer and wave banners. You're here to break the record for the highest motorcycle jump ever.

The ramp in front of you shoots nearly straight up and is ready to launch you into thin air. You double-check your bike and your safety equipment. You need speed to do this right. Revving your engine, you start for the ramp to do an easy practice jump. It's perfect. One more for good measure, and then you hit the *throttle*, pushing your bike to the limit.

You hit the ramp and soar up into the air. You turn the bike down toward the landing ramp and return to ground, landing safely. You did it! It's a brand new world record. You just jumped higher than anyone ever has before!

quarter pipe—a ramp with a slightly convex surface, used by motorcyclists to perform jumps and other maneuvers

throttle—a lever, pedal, or handle used to control the speed of an engine

5

The Early Days of Motorcycles and Stunts

Born to Push Limits

In 1867 Sylvester H. Roper developed a bicycle-like machine that ran using steam power. The frame was made of wood, and the wheels were wood and iron. Roper lived in Massachusetts and demonstrated his new invention up and down the East Coast at fairs and circuses. In 1885 German inventor Gottlieb Daimler improved upon this design with the first gasoline-powered motorcycle. From that point on, motorcycles have continued to improve.

Gottlieb Daimler's motorcycle from 1885

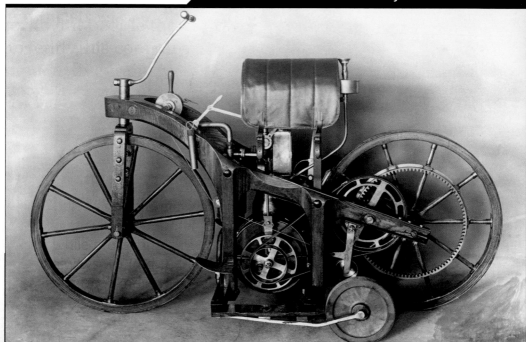

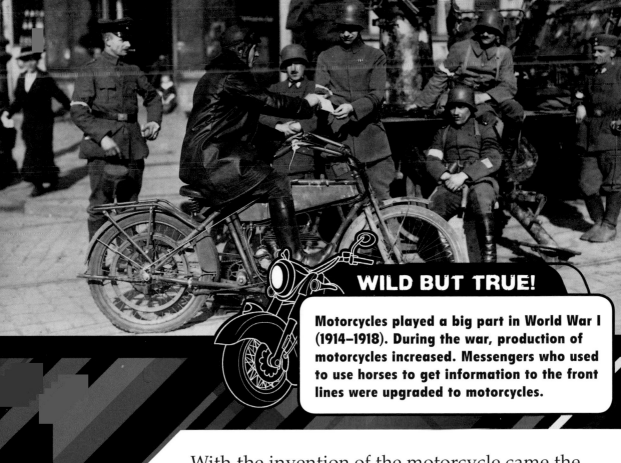

WILD BUT TRUE!

Motorcycles played a big part in World War I (1914–1918). During the war, production of motorcycles increased. Messengers who used to use horses to get information to the front lines were upgraded to motorcycles.

With the invention of the motorcycle came the desire to push its limits. Orren "Putt" Mossman was a *motorcycle stuntman* who bought his first motorcycle in 1926. As he drove it home, he stood on the seat to impress two young ladies. They clapped for him, and an idea was born. He could do motorcycle tricks to make money. Soon Mossman was performing jumps, each bigger than the last. Mossman hired more riders and formed a *troupe* that traveled the country performing their stunts.

motorcycle stuntman—a person who performs special skills involving acrobatic maneuvering of the bike and sometimes the rider; common maneuvers include wheelies, stoppies, and burnouts

troupe—a group of motorcyclists or other entertainers who tour to different venues

Early Motorcycle Daredevils

Nick DeRush was a movie stuntman in the 1930s. When not working on a film, he liked to take his Harley Davidson motorcycle to the pier. There, he would ask people if they'd like to see him ride off of the end of the dock. People loved to watch his unusual performance. Soon Nick and his friends became a traveling motorcycle stunt show.

As early as 1927, a team of horse and motorcycle stunt riders from Yorkshire, England, began demonstrating stunts. The team, known as the White Helmets, is still intact today with as many as 30 riders.

Nick DeRush on his motorcycle

The White Helmets stunt team is comprised of men and women serving in the British Royal Corps of Signals. The British Royal Corps of Signals is a branch of the British Army.

People enjoy the daring and unusual tricks that can be performed with motorcycles. Each stunt rider wants to hold a wheelie the longest, jump the highest, and go faster than ever.

Elements of the Motorcycle Stunt

Early on, there were few types of motorcycles, so riders would use similar models. Different styles evolved over time. Today, manufacturers make some bikes heavy for long, comfortable rides. Others, called sport bikes, are made for speed and performance. These are the bikes that push the limits of stunts.

Wheelies and *stoppies* require bikes with balance and strong brakes. While most bikes use a foot brake, many stunt bikes also have a hand brake to allow the rider to have better control. Extra brake *calipers* on the wheels help to increase the braking efficiency.

Stunt bikes might have added pegs as a place for riders to place their feet during tricks. Rear seats, *fenders*, and even gas tanks can be altered. This allows the rider to stand up during a stunt. A 12 o'clock bar can be added to the rear of the bike for the bike to rest on while doing a wheelie.

stoppie—a trick in which the back wheel is lifted and the bike is ridden on the front wheel by carefully applying brake pressure

calipers—a set of clamps at the end of a brake cable that press against a wheel's rim to stop the wheel from turning

fender—a covering over a motorcycle wheel that protects the wheel from damage

CHECK THIS OUT! Some riders have special rear fenders that drag on the ground during wheelies and send sparks shooting into the air behind them.

Bikes That Fly

For *aerial* stunts such as jumps and freestyle acrobatics, riders need very light bikes. This allows them to *maneuver* in mid-air. Options such as kickstands, electric starters, and headlights are not installed on these bikes to keep weight down. Seats are often shaved down to create easier movement for the rider. Rear fenders are usually removed so they're not in the way during tricks.

aerial—a trick that is done in the air

maneuver—a planned and controlled movement that requires practiced skills

Most riders prefer a bike with a *two-stroke engine*. It has more power than its four-stroke counterpart. Because of the extreme jumping these bikes do, they also need super-strength *suspension systems*. Suspension helps absorb the shock when the bike and the rider land on the ground after a jump. Crash cages and subcages are pieces of metal added to the bikes to protect the engine and the frame.

WILD BUT TRUE!

In 2014 motorcycle jumper Gary Davis decided to sell his collection of motorcycles. His collection was made up of mostly racing bikes. By the time he decided to sell off his collection, he had more than 200 motorcycles in his garage.

two-stroke engine—a gas engine that completes a power cycle in just two strokes, or up and down movements of the pistons

suspension system—a system of springs and shock absorbers connecting the main body of a vehicle to the wheels and axles

The Tools of the Trade

While many stunts only require the rider and the bike itself, there are many other pieces of equipment that can play a part.

Ramps are essential for jumps. There are many styles of ramps, each designed for a specific jump. Some are for distance while others are shaped to provide height for freestyle tricks. Some riders jump over other things as well. Cars, buses, flaming hoops, and even moving trains have all been obstacles for motorcycle jumpers.

In 2009 Robbie Maddison used the London Tower Bridge as a ramp. After jumping the gap between drawbridges, Maddison said, "It was an incredible feeling to fly between the two towers and over the Thames [River]."

Some riders use a large metal sphere to ride in circles and even upside down. Sometimes they'll even put several riders into one sphere creating a dizzying whir of motion.

Stunts that aim for speed records need a precise radar gun to record the speed of the bike. For timed events such as holding a wheelie, officials may use a stopwatch.

Using a ramp, this stunt driver jumps through a flaming hoop.

Preparing for the Worst

For every motorcycle stunt, there are dangers involved. Proper safety equipment and procedures are crucial to a successful stunt. Riders use helmets to protect their heads in case of a fall. They protect their elbows and knees with extra pads and braces. Fire can be a major hazard in a stunt. Many riders wear special fire suits designed to protect them from heat and flames.

Some jumps require safety nets to catch the rider in case of a fall. Special padded walls provide safe barriers if riders cannot stop their bikes where they land.

Safety gear is not the only way to keep riders safe. By knowing the necessary speeds and angles for various stunts, riders can perform stunts more successfully. It takes pro stunt riders years of training to learn how to master their tricks.

CHECK THIS OUT! Performing wheelies on public roads is illegal in most countries, including in the United States.

Stuntmen and Stuntwomen of Note

Evel Unparalleled

When it comes to motorcycle stunts, one name stands out above the rest: Evel Knievel. Between 1965 and 1980 Knievel attempted more than 75 spectacular jumps. With his fancy leather jumpsuits and cape, he mesmerized crowds with his amazing jumps. He once jumped over 22 parked cars. He also made jumps over Greyhound buses, pits of rattlesnakes, and even a pool with 13 sharks.

On New Year's Eve 1967 he attempted to jump the fountains at Caesar's Palace in Las Vegas, Nevada, but failed. He was injured in the crash. Knievel suffered 433 broken bones over the course of his career. Knievel's Harley Davidson XR-750 motorcycle is on display at the Smithsonian National Museum of American History. During his career Knievel consistently spoke about motorcycle safety—especially the importance of wearing a helmet.

WILD BUT TRUE!

Evel Knievel's son, Robbie, followed in his father's footsteps as a stunt rider. At age four he was jumping his bicycle. By age seven he was riding a motorcycle. In 1989 Robbie successfully jumped the Fountains at Caesar's Palace in honor of his father.

"Anybody can jump a motorcycle.
The trouble begins when you try to land it."
Evel Knievel

The Best on Bikes

When a great rider lands a new stunt, there is always a desire to do something bigger and better. Today's top stunt riders compete with each other to pull off the most insane tricks.

Robbie "Maddo" Maddison is an Australian rider who lives to push the limits. He's set world records for longest ramp jump several times and was even a *stunt double* for James Bond in *Skyfall*.

Carey Hart invented a trick called the Hart Attack. It's where a rider puts one hand on the seat and the other hand on the handlebar and does a handstand. All while in mid-air!

Carey Hart performs the Hart Attack.

stunt double—a person who takes the place of an actress or actor in an action scene or when a special skill or great risk is called for

Travis Pastrana does a double backflip.

The X Games is one of the premier stages for freestyle stunt riders. Travis Pastrana was the first to land a double backflip in competition at the X Games. He won his first X Games gold medal at age 15. Mike Metzger, another X Games champ, once did a motorcycle backflip over the fountains at Caesar's Palace. Brian Deegan has tallied more X Games medals than any other rider. As of 2014 he had 13 medals.

CHECK THIS OUT!

Freestyle was not considered an official sport for many years. In 1998 the Freestyle Motocross Association was created to establish rules for the sport.

Daring Women

Motorcycle stunt riding does not belong to men alone. Throughout history several women have excelled at stunt riding. In 1939 Theresa Wallach became the first woman to receive the British Motorcycle Racing Club's Gold Star. She got it for averaging more than 100 miles (161 kilometers) per hour on the famous Brooklands circuit. Bessie "BB" Stringfield performed hill-climbing stunts and trick riding in carnival stunt shows in the United States. She even served as a motorcycle dispatch rider during World War II (1939–1945).

Today, even more women are hopping on bikes. At just 18 years old, Debbie Evans jumped a motorcycle over a 30-foot (9-meter) ravine for a movie scene. That stunt sparked a Hall of Fame career doing both car and motorcycle stunts for the movies. At just 5-foot-2 (1.56 m) and 113 pounds (51 kilograms), Jessica Maine goes by the nickname Smallz. Maine is a pioneer for women's wheelies competitions and exhibitions.

CHECK THIS OUT!

Ashley Fiolek is deaf stunt rider in the Marvel's Universe Live Show. She learned to ride in the woods at her grandfather's cabin in Wolverine, Michigan.

Ashley Fiolek

Famous Motorcycle Stunts

Some stunts are impressive. Others are so wild and imaginative that they become legendary.

Ten-Story Drop

On New Year's Eve 2008 Robbie Maddison jumped from a ramp to the top of a 10-story building in Las Vegas. From there he proceeded to ride off of the roof to land safely on another ramp.

"Even if you paid me $10 million, I'd never do it again."

Robbie Maddison, on his "Ten-Story Drop" stunt

Grand Canyon Jump

Robbie Knievel jumped over a portion of the Grand Canyon, clearing 228 feet (69 m). The depth of the canyon at the jump site was 2,500 feet (762 m) deep. He crashed and broke his leg on the landing.

Great Wall Jump

In 1993 Eddie Kidd jumped his motorcycle over the Great Wall of China. Kidd did motorcycle stunts in many movies, including the 1981 film *Riding High*.

WILD BUT TRUE!

In 1975 "Super" Joe Einhorn vowed to jump Niagara Falls on a rocket-powered motorcycle. However, he suffered a head injury during a jump at *Santa Fe Speedway* in Willow Springs, Illinois, before he could try to tackle Niagara Falls.

Jumping Out of the Big Screen

Motorcycle stunts make for memorable scenes on the big screen. Check out some of the most amazing movie stunts done on two wheels.

Terminator 2 — Stuntman Bob Brown, as "T-1000," took a 190-foot (58-m) starting run to crash his Kawasaki 650 through a window. Brown flew through broken glass before a safety cable caught him and lowered him onto a safety pad.

Bob Brown crashes through a window in *Terminator 2*.

"It's like your body is saying, 'Get me out of here!' But you've got to tell yourself, 'I'm going to go through that window, and nobody's going to see me blink.'"
Bob Brown, on his jump in the movie *Terminator 2*

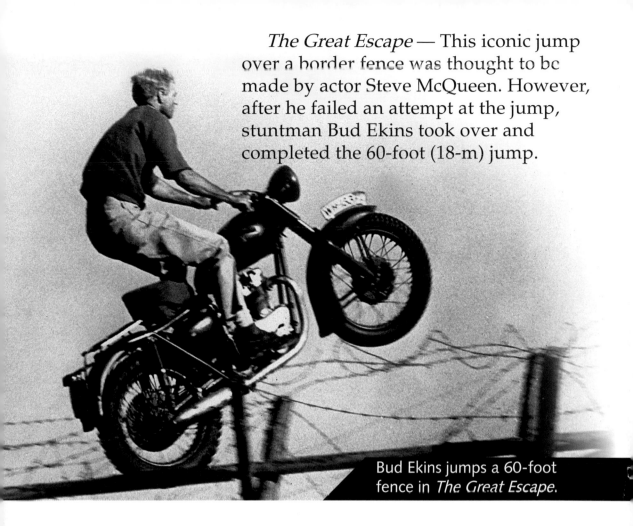

The Great Escape — This iconic jump over a border fence was thought to be made by actor Steve McQueen. However, after he failed an attempt at the jump, stuntman Bud Ekins took over and completed the 60-foot (18-m) jump.

Bud Ekins jumps a 60-foot fence in *The Great Escape*.

Tomorrow Never Dies — In a dramatic chase scene, James Bond escapes a pursuing helicopter on a BMW motorcycle. Stuntman Jean Pierre also had a passenger sitting across his lap. The exciting scene took three weeks to film and finished with a motorcycle jump over the helicopter.

WILD BUT TRUE!

Long-time stunt innovator Dar Robinson had never broken a bone in his 19-year Hollywood career. However, he was killed while filming a routine high-speed chase scene on the set of *Million Dollar Mystery* on November 21, 1986.

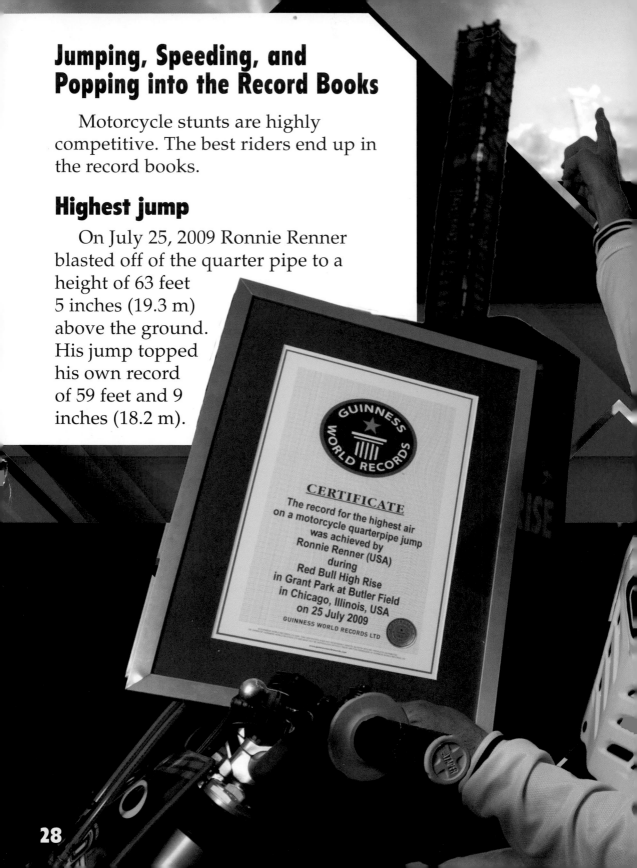

Jumping, Speeding, and Popping into the Record Books

Motorcycle stunts are highly competitive. The best riders end up in the record books.

Highest jump

On July 25, 2009 Ronnie Renner blasted off of the quarter pipe to a height of 63 feet 5 inches (19.3 m) above the ground. His jump topped his own record of 59 feet and 9 inches (18.2 m).

GUINNESS WORLD RECORDS

CERTIFICATE

The record for the highest air on a motorcycle quarterpipe jump was achieved by
Ronnie Renner (USA)
during
Red Bull High Rise
in Grant Park at Butler Field
in Chicago, Illinois, USA
on 25 July 2009

GUINNESS WORLD RECORDS LTD

Longest Ramp Jump

Ryan Capes sailed with his bike through the air for an astounding 390 feet (119 m). That's like flying over the distance of a football field.

Wheelie

Riding a wheelie for a few feet can be dangerous enough. Japanese rider Yasuyuki Kudo rode his bike with one wheel up for an amazing 205.7 miles (331 km). That's an amazing feat of balance and strength.

Fastest Motorcycle

Rocky Robinson drove a specially *streamlined* motorcycle to break the world record with a speed of 376 miles (605 km) per hour. Typical airplanes cruise at 575 miles (925 km) per hour.

CHECK THIS OUT! Patrick Furstenhoff holds the record for the highest speed reached on one wheel with his 191.3 miles (307.9 km) per hour wheelie.

streamlined—if a vehicle is streamlined, it is designed so that it can move through air or water very quickly and easily

Glossary

aerial (AYR-ee-uhl)—a trick that is done in the air

calipers (KA-luh-puhrz)—a set of clamps at the end of a brake cable that press against a wheel's rim to stop the wheel from turning

fender (FEN-duhr)—a covering over a motorcycle wheel that protects the wheel from damage

maneuver (muh-NOO-ver)—a planned and controlled movement that requires practiced skills

motorcycle stuntman (MOH-tur-sye-kuhl STUHNT-man)—a person who performs special skills involving acrobatic maneuvering of the bike and sometimes the rider; common maneuvers include wheelies, stoppies, and burnouts

quarter pipe (KWOR-tur PIPE)—a ramp with a slightly convex surface, used by motorcyclists to perform jumps and other maneuvers

stoppie (STOP-pee)—a trick in which the back wheel is lifted and the bike is ridden on the front wheel by carefully applying brake pressure

streamlined (STREEM-lined)—if a vehicle is streamlined, it is designed so that it can move through air or water very quickly and easily

stunt double (STUHNT DUH-buhl)—a person who takes the place of an actress or actor in an action scene or when a special skill or great risk is called for

suspension system (suh-SPEN-shuhn SISS-tuhm)—a system of springs and shock absorbers connecting the main body of a vehicle to the wheels and axles

throttle (THROT-uhl)—a lever, pedal, or handle used to control the speed of an engine

troupe (TROOP)—a group of motorcyclists or other entertainers who tour to different venues

two-stroke engine (TOO-strohk EN-juhn)—a gas engine that completes a power cycle in just two strokes, or up and down movements of the pistons

Read More

Brooklyn, Billie B. *Motorcycle Racing.* Checkered Flag. New York: PowerKids Press, 2015.

Catel, Patrick. *Surviving Stunts and Other Amazing Feats.* Extreme Survival. Chicago. Raintree, 2011.

Polydoros, Lori. *Motocross Greats.* Best of the Best. Mankato, Minn.: Capstone Press, 2012.

Internet Sites

FactHound offers a safe, fun way to find Internet sites related to this book. All of the sites on FactHound have been researched by our staff.

Here's all you do:

Visit *www.facthound.com*

Type in this code: 9781491442555

 Check out projects, games and lots more at **www.capstonekids.com**

Index